Can you find the owls?

There are 6 species of owl living in the wild in the United Kingdom. Can you find them all in this story?

Little Owl

Barn Owl

Brown (Tawny) Owl

Long-eared Owl

Eagle Owl

Short-eared Owl

For the amazing Jen and Nise - KP
For Ana and Sofie and my godchildren Evie, Jasmine and little Tyler, with special thanks to Korbyn for being a super model - SR

'May we all enjoy, cherish and protect our glorious countryside and precious wildlife, the future of which is in our hands.'

Published by KAMA Publishing
19A The Swale, Norwich, NR5 9HE
www.kamapublishing.co.uk

First printed 2016

British Library Cataloguing in Publication Data. A catalogue record for this book is available from the British Library.

Paperback ISBN 9780956719683
Hardback ISBN 9780956719690

Printed in the European Union

One Fine Summer's Night

To Isabel,

With best wishes

By
Kevin Price

Illustrated by
Sarah Reilly

Enjoy our wonderful wildlife!

9/6/2019

One fine summer's night, when a full moon shone bright
and the twinkling of stars filled the sky,
I quietly stood, at the edge of the wood,
making notes of the things that passed by.

I picked up my pen at a quarter to ten,
when I spotted a nervous young fox.
She sniffed at the air and she quietly stared,
as she watched her cubs play on some rocks.

At twenty past ten they went back to their den
and I waited in silence once more.
As I waited there, small black shapes filled the
air and I counted them; one, two, three, four.

They were pipistrelle bats that were out catching gnats
and they flittered and fluttered away.
You can see them in flight only during the night,
as they hang upside down through the day.

At ten past eleven I saw Mr Bevan,
who walked round the lake with his dogs.
They started to bark, as they heard through the dark,
noisy croaking from hundreds of frogs.

As midnight drew near I spied
two fallow deer that were grazing
on tender young shoots.
They searched all around, through
the leaves on the ground, for the
wind-fallen berries and fruits.

At twenty to one they broke into a run and
they scurried off into the trees.
They'd been startled and scared and so off
they'd both hared when the tree branches
swayed in the breeze.

At quarter to two something cried, ‘Twit twoo’,
then I saw it swoop down to the ground.

The stealthy brown owl which had let out the howl
was now eating the mouse it had found.

At just after three, in the ferns next to me,
something sniffled and snuffled and scrunched.
It was eating a bug, or a succulent slug
and it rustled the leaves as it munched.
A nettle sting burned as I parted the ferns
that were growing beneath a great pine.
And what did I see at the base of the tree?
A small hedgehog all covered in spines.

At twenty past three something flew around me,
then it settled upon my shirt cloth.
I looked down to see what this creature could be -
a magnificent cinnabar moth.

The moth flew away at the break of the day
and I heard the farm's cock give a crow.
The dawn's early light marked the end of
the night; it was nearly time for me to go.

I took a last look, then I picked up my book
and I set off for home with regret.
I'd waited all night and I'd hoped to catch sight
of a creature I hadn't seen yet.

I walked down the lane, then looked backwards again
and I thought that I saw a dark shape.
I opened my book as I went back to look -
it was using its front legs to scrape.

I saw black and white in the early dawn light
and now I was as pleased as could be,
for the animal there with the black and white hair
was the badger that I'd hoped to see.

I made my way back down the dusty farm track
and I reached home at just after four.
I climbed into bed and I laid down my head
and in no time I started to snore.

I know it may seem when you're having your dreams
that the rest of the world sleeps with you,
but when day turns to night and the moon shines its light
then the cycle of life starts anew.

At the end of the day creatures come out to play,
while the rest of the world goes to sleep.
Maybe one day you might stay awake through the night
for some memories you'll always keep.

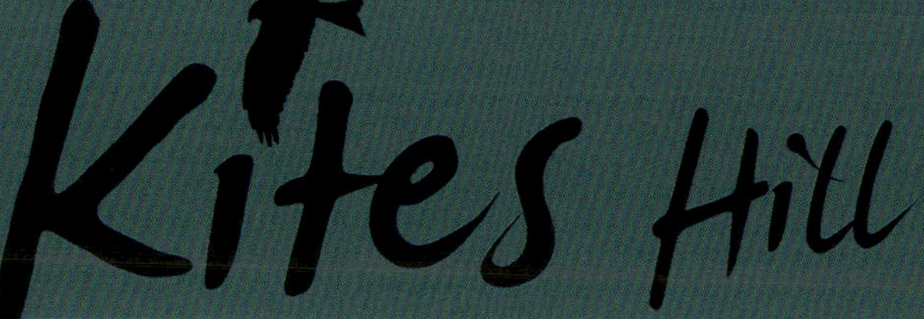

About World Land Trust

World Land Trust (WLT), whose Patrons include Sir David Attenborough, Chris Packham and Steve Backshall, has been saving animals and their habitats since 1989. More than 500,000 acres of wildlife habitat has been saved so far and land is being purchased and protected acre by acre as funds are raised.

WLT works with 30 overseas conservation partner organisations in 20 different countries, saving threatened tropical forests and other vital habitats. The Trust has one project area in the UK: Kites Hill, in Gloucestershire.

The Kites Hill Reserve

Kites Hill Reserve is a Special Area for Conservation. The beautiful native woodland with its ancient beech trees is a paradise for plant, animal and bird species. WLT has provided breeding sites (including nest boxes and stacks of wood) throughout the Reserve for butterflies, bats, owls and other species that had previously disappeared from the area. A pond has been created which is now attracting invertebrates and other pond life. Interpretation boards have been installed along the nature trail for visitors to learn about the conservation of the reserve.

Thank you for your donation

All donations resulting from the sale of this book will be used to conserve the Kites Hill Reserve.

World Land Trust is a registered charity No. 1001291.
For information please contact:
World Land Trust, Blyth House, Bridge Street, Halesworth, Suffolk IP19 8AB

Telephone: 01986 874422
Email: info@worldlandtrust.org

Saving Real Acres in Real Places

www.worldlandtrust.org

ANIMAL FACTS

Fox Facts

- Foxes have whiskers on their legs which they use to help find their way in the dark.
- They are a great night-time predator because their eyes are specially adapted to night vision.
- Their eyes have two cell layers, which doubles the intensity of images that the fox receives. They also glow green when light is shone into them at night.
- Foxes have become a common sight in urban areas. This is because they can adapt their diet to live off the waste that humans produce. Do you have any living near you?

Bat Facts

- There are 18 species of bat living in the United Kingdom
- Britain's most common (and smallest) bat is called the pipistrelle. One individual can eat over 3000 insects in a single night, even though they weigh less than a pound coin!
- In winter, bats go into a deep sleep called hibernation.
- Blind as a bat? Bats actually have good eyesight, much like a human, although at night their ears are far more important. They use a sonar system called echolocation to find their way around, emitting high-pitched sounds and listening for them to 'bounce off' objects, such as flying insects. These sounds are too high for most human ears to hear, although sometimes children can hear them. Can you?
- Bats are warm blooded and are the only mammals that can fly.
- Bats roost upside down so they are ready to take flight. Their claws hold on tight while they are asleep.
- Bat populations have declined in the past century, as changes in land use mean that there are less insects to feed on, but conservation trusts are working hard to protect them.
- Bats' knees can bend backwards!

Frog Facts

- There are 2 species of frog living in the United Kingdom; the Common Frog and the Pool Frog. There are also 2 species of their close relative, the toad; the Common Toad and the Natterjack Toad.
- Frogs are amphibians, which means that they can survive in water and on dry land.
- They will die if their skin dries out as it absorbs water, which maintains their body temperature.

- Their skin can contain toxic substances. Some species of frog living in South America are so poisonous that their secretions can kill humans.
- Frogs can see forwards, sideways and upwards, all at the same time. Most species also have a good sense of hearing.
- Frogs like to sleep, usually during the daytime.
- Some species of frog protect themselves against predators by camouflaging themselves. Some can even change their skin colour to match their environment.
- All frogs have hind legs that are longer and stronger than their front limbs, which makes them excellent jumpers and swimmers.

ANIMAL FACTS

Owl Facts

- There are 6 species of owl living in the United Kingdom; Barn, Brown (also known as Tawny), Little, Long-eared, Short-eared and Eagle. Eagle owls have only recently been re-introduced.
- Owls are carnivorous (meat-eating) and their main food in the UK is small rodents, such as mice, shrews and voles, although they will occasionally catch small birds, insects and frogs.
- Nocturnal owls catch their prey by using their incredible hearing. For example, a barn owl can find a mouse in total darkness if it makes the smallest of noises.
- Not all owls are nocturnal. Little and short-eared hunt mostly during the day.
- Owls' eyes are fixed in position. This means that if they want to look at something which isn't directly in front of them then they have to move their whole head. Amazingly, an owl's head can turn through 280 degrees – this is nearly the whole way round!
- Unlike many other birds, owls' feathers aren't waterproof, so they can't hunt when it's raining.
- If you are walking in an area where owls live, you may find 'pellets' filled with bones, fur and skin. These are the bits of animals that owls can't digest, which they regurgitate and spit out.

Deer Facts

- There are 6 species of deer living in the United Kingdom; Red, Roe, Fallow, Sika, Reeve's Muntjac and Chinese Water. Only red deer and roe deer are native to our islands, but some consider fallow deer as now being native, having been originally introduced as long ago as the 11th century by the Normans.
- In all deer species (except reindeer) only the male has antlers. These are shed in Spring and a new set immediately grows, taking around 16 weeks to reach their full size.
- Antlers are used to fight other males in the breeding season. This is called the 'rut' and usually takes place in late Autumn.
- There are more deer in the South of England today than there were 500 years ago.
- All deer are herbivores (plant-eating), living mainly on grass, shrubs, berries, seeds and even tree bark.

ANIMAL FACTS

Hedgehog Facts

- Hedgehogs are nocturnal, so they mainly come out at night and sleep during the day.
- They make nests in and forage through undergrowth, using their long snouts to find food.
- Their eyes are specially adapted for night time vision and their eyesight is extremely poor in daytime.
- They have around 5000 spines, which last for about a year and then drop out and regrow.
- Baby hedgehogs are born blind and their spines are soft.
- When threatened hedgehogs roll into a tight, prickly ball with their sharp spines protecting them against predators.
- Like bats, hedgehogs hibernate in the winter.
- Gardeners like hedgehogs, as their favourite foods are slugs and snails.

Moth Facts

- There are around 2500 species of moth found in the United Kingdom. Most are native, but some have found their way here from continental Europe.
- Unlike their cousins, the butterflies, moths are nocturnal, although you may accidentally disturb one during the day.
- Moths are attracted to bright lights, as in the wild they use the Moon for navigation.
- Cinnabar Moths are common throughout the United Kingdom. Their caterpillars are very distinctive, having bright yellow and black stripes.

Badger Facts

- Badgers are fully nocturnal and rather elusive.
- They are very clean animals and live in complex underground burrow systems called setts. Some setts are centuries old and may have several chambers, including separate toilets! They often have a number of tunnels leading to the surface.
- Badgers spend around 70% of their lives underground.
- They are excellent diggers, their claws, streamlined body shape and muscular frames being specially adapted for this purpose. Their name is believed to come from the French word, 'becheur', which means 'to dig'.
- Badgers can eat several hundred earthworms in a single night and they also enjoy insects, bluebell bulbs and elderberries.
- Like humans, they have five toes.
- Badgers are protected in England by the wildlife and countryside act 1982 and protection of badgers act 1992.